ROTHERHAM LIBRARY & INFORMATION SERVICES

BRITAIN IN WORLD WAR II

Evacuation

Margaret Stephen

Based on an original text by
Fiona Reynoldson

WAYLAND

BRITAIN IN WORLD WAR II
Titles in this series
THE BLITZ
EVACUATION

Editor: Jason Hook
Original Design: Nick Cannan
Differentiated Design: Raynor Design
Cover Design: Giles Wheeler
Text Consultant: Norah Granger, University of Brighton

Based on an original text *The Home Front – Evacuation*, by Fiona Reynoldson, published in 1990 by Wayland Publishers Limited

First published in 1998 by Wayland Publishers Limited, 61 Western Road, Hove, East Sussex BN3 1JD
© Copyright 1998 Wayland Publishers Limited

Find Wayland on the Internet at http//www.wayland.co.uk

British Library Cataloguing in Publication Data
Stephen, Margaret
  Evacuation. – (Britain in World War II)
  1. World War, 1939-1945 – Evacuation of civilians – Great Britain – Juvenile literature
  I. Title
  940.5'3161'0941

ISBN 0 7502 2285 9

Typeset in England by Raynor Design
Printed and bound by G. Canale & CSpA, Turin
Cover picture: Children being evacuated by train from London.

 See page 31 for ways in which you can use this book to encourage literacy skills.

Acknowledgements
The quotes in this book were taken from the following sources: Dennis Baker, Birmingham (p. 7); Michael Aspel (p. 11), Bryan Griffiths (p. 19), H. Cuthbert (p. 25) in *The Evacuees* by B.S. Johnson; David Gurr (p. 12), Alan Burrell (p. 13), Patricia Ferman (p. 13), (p. 16) in *No Time to Wave Goodbye* by Ben Wicks; a boy aged 10 in *Children of the Blitz* by Robert Westall (p. 15); Jane Clarke, Manchester (p. 17); *Town Children Through Country Eyes*, a Women's Institute Report (p. 21); Lil Lawrence, Kent (p. 23); J.M. Turner, Kent (p. 24); *Flight in the Winter* by Juergen Thorwald (p. 29).

The publishers would like to thank the following for permission to reproduce their pictures: ET Archives Limited 5 (top); Getty Images *cover*; Imperial War Museum 5 (bottom), 7, 9, 15 (top), 20 (both), 22 (bottom), 24, 28, 29 (top); John Frost 13 (top); Mary Evans 15 (bottom); Peter Newark's Historical Pictures 25 (top); Popperfoto 10 (bottom), 12, 14, 16, 17 (top), 19 (top), 21, 22 (top), 27 (top); Topham 6 (both), 8 (top), 10 (top), 11, 13 (bottom), 18, 19 (bottom), 23, 25 (bottom), 26, 27 (bottom); Wayland Picture Library 17 (bottom); Weimar Archive 8 (bottom), 29 (bottom). The artwork on page 4 is by Peter Bull Art Studio.

Contents

The Fear of War

Adolf Hitler became the leader of Germany in 1933. He wanted to make Germany a strong country again.

In Britain, people were worried that Hitler would start a war in Europe. German aeroplanes might drop bombs on Britain.

German planes based in France would be able to fly over Britain and bomb it. But Britain did not have many planes which could fly far enough to bomb big German cities such as Berlin.

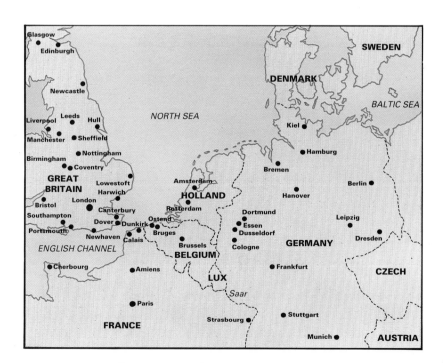

▶ German planes based in France could bomb London.

EVACUATION

◄ Hitler built up a large army. This made people afraid that Germany would invade.

▼ Signposts in Britain were taken away. If the Germans invaded, they would not be able to find their way around.

The first plans

Winston Churchill wrote about the German air force in a letter to his wife in 1933: 'There is no doubt that the Germans are already stronger than us in the air.'

In Britain, the government began to plan how to get people out of the cities to be safe if there was a war. They were planning an 'evacuation'.

Evacuation in Britain

▲ A government poster telling people about evacuation.

London is the largest city in Britain. Plans were made for many people to be evacuated from London to the countryside. They left on trains from big London stations.

Most evacuees were children over five years of age. Mothers with children under five were also evacuated.

▶ Children shelter from an attack by German planes.

Safe in the country

Evacuees were sent from all big cities to safe areas in the countryside. They would be safe there if the cities were bombed.

One evacuee from Birmingham said: 'I and five other boys were sent to the country estate of the Fry family – the chocolate people. We lived there helping on the farm for the rest of the war.'

No one had to be evacuated if they did not want to be. But parents wanted their children to be away from danger.

—— In France and Germany ——

▲ Some people who had been treated badly in Germany escaped to Britain when the war started.

World War II started in 1939. In Germany, people in danger were quickly evacuated to safer places. Many were moved away from the border between Germany and France.

The Maginot Line

The French had built a line of forts along the border to protect their country from the Germans. It was called the Maginot Line.

Many thousands of French evacuees left their homes near the Maginot Line. They travelled across France in trains. Their journey was long and tiring.

▶ The German army leads an evacuation.

When the French evacuees arrived, they had to sleep in other people's houses. Some of them even slept in barns or cowsheds.

The German army went round the Maginot Line to get to Paris. People rushed to leave Paris in any transport they could find.

▼ French people try to escape before the German army arrives.

Getting Ready

▲ A boy with his belongings, waiting to be evacuated.

In Britain, the government gave out a leaflet to parents. It told them all about evacuation. The leaflet had a list of cities and towns in England and Scotland. These places had to be evacuated.

Headteachers made up registers of the children who had to be evacuated from their schools.

▶ A family reading a list of clothes an evacuee will need.

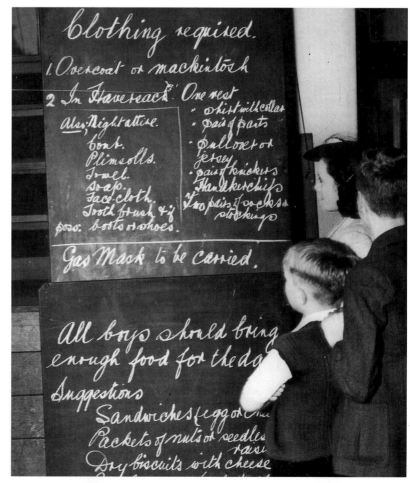

Parents had to pack cases for their children. A teacher wrote on the blackboard a list of the things that evacuees needed. They needed to take clothes, soap and a toothbrush.

▲ Children being evacuated from Kent. They are wearing labels and carrying their gas masks in boxes.

The children leave

Children marched with their teachers along the streets to the railway station. The children carried gas masks and wore big labels.

One of these children wrote: 'People stood on their doorsteps to watch us pass and shopkeepers gave us sweets, and packets of nuts and raisins.'

Saying Goodbye

At schools and railway stations all over the country, mothers and fathers said goodbye to their children. Some parents cried. They were very worried about German bombs. They were frightened that they would never see their children again.

One child wrote: 'My dad suddenly vanished, he left us in the middle of the school yard. He couldn't bear to be in the hall of the school with us, so he just walked away so he wouldn't break down and cry in front of us.'

▼ Parents and their children saying goodbye at a railway station.

◀ After Germany defeated France, this newspaper asked all parents to evacuate their children.

Some children were excited. Evacuation seemed like holiday time. The children did not understand the dangers.

Gas masks

All the evacuees carried their gas masks. No one liked wearing a gas mask. Years later, one woman remembered how it felt: 'The awful choking sensation and sweating inside that rubber mask.'

▲ Pupils get ready to leave with their teacher.

Going Away

Many evacuees did not enjoy their journey to the country. They spent all day on trains. Some were sick. Some could not get to the toilet because the trains had no corridors.

▼ Schoolboys leaving London by train.

It was dark when the evacuees arrived. They were tired and hungry. They were given hot drinks, sandwiches and biscuits.

One boy remembered: 'Some children treated it as a great adventure, others quietly sobbed.'

Finding a home

Foster parents chose children to take to their homes. They were paid to look after the evacuees. But it was difficult to find homes for the hundreds of children who arrived on the trains. Homes also had to be found for the children's teachers.

▲ Officials checking lists of evacuees arriving in Devon.

▼ An advertisement for foster parents.

YOUR EVACUEES!
Extra mouths to feed
To make the most and get the best out of every scrap of meat
use
BISTO

Being Chosen

After their long journey, evacuees were taken to wait in a big hall. Here, foster parents were allowed to choose the children they wanted in their homes.

The first children chosen by foster parents were often the good-looking ones or the quiet ones.

▼ Evacuees waiting to be chosen by foster parents.

One girl wrote about how evacuees felt as they waited to be picked: 'We felt like cattle at an auction.'

◀ These children have just met their foster parents.

Children who were not chosen felt sad and unwanted. They were taken from house to house to try to find them a home. Some children were so unhappy, they even tried to walk home to London.

Children from the same family wanted to stay together. One boy wrote about waiting to be picked with his brother and sister: 'People came in and picked other children all around us. But none wanted the three of us.'

▼ A poster asking for more foster parents.

Thank you, Foster-Parents . . . we want more like you!

Some kindly folk have been looking after children from the cities for over six months. Extra work? Yes, they've been a handful! . . . but the foster-parents know they have done the right thing.

And think of all the people who have cause to be thanking the foster-parents. First, the children themselves. They're out of a danger-zone — where desperate peril may come at any minute. And they're healthier and happier. Perhaps they don't say it but they certainly mean "Thank you".

Then their parents. Think what it means to them!

The Government are grateful to all the 20,000 people in Scotland who are so greatly helping the country by looking after evacuated children. But many new volunteers are needed—to share in the present task and to be ready for any crisis that may come. Won't you be one of them? All you need do is enrol your name with the local Authority. You will be doing a real service for the nation. You may be saving a child's life.

The Secretary of State, who has been entrusted by the Government with the conduct of evacuation, asks you urgently to join the Roll of those who are willing to receive children. Please apply to your local Council.

Away from Home

Foster homes were all different. Many children were taken into nice homes with kind foster parents. Some enjoyed country life on farms among fields and woods. They had never seen places like this.

▼ Many evacuees enjoyed helping on farms.

At first, many evacuees were homesick. But soon they made friends in their new homes and villages.

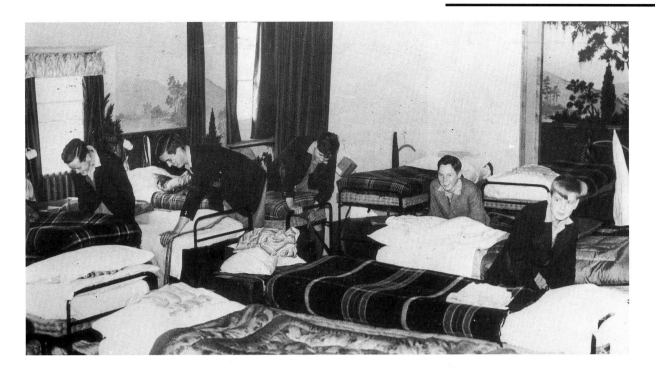

Some evacuees were very unhappy. For the first time in their lives, some boys and girls met people who hated them. A brother and sister were thrown out of their foster home just because they were Jewish.

▲ These evacuees used a hotel as their foster home.

Happy homes

One Welsh evacuee liked his foster home better than his own home: 'There I had shared a bed with my two brothers, gone shoeless and lived on dry toast and dripping. This was another life – fresh country food, a room of my own.'

▼ Evacuees having fun.

Homesick Children

Evacuees were often homesick. Many of them wet their beds because they were so unhappy. Some foster parents did not understand. They punished children for bed-wetting. Sometimes children were hit or even locked in a cupboard.

▼ A poster asking mothers to leave their children in the country.

▼ Evacuees from London.

Children were homesick because their parents could not visit them. Fathers were away fighting in the war. Mothers worked in factories. Most parents did not have cars and it was expensive to travel by train.

▲ Happy children run to meet their parents.

Problems for foster parents

Some foster parents were shocked by their evacuees. Some children arrived with head lice and body lice. Other children brought no change of underwear with them.

A report about evacuees from Manchester said: 'Some children had never slept in beds. One boy had never had a bath.'

Mothers

Many mothers with children under five were evacuated with their children. Their husbands were away fighting in the army, navy or air force.

Mothers were evacuated on trains, just like the schoolchildren. They travelled from cities like London to the countryside.

Some mothers from the cities found it difficult to live in the countryside. They missed entertainments like the cinema, and found country life too quiet.

▲ Mothers and their children leave London.

▶ Women in the city going to the cinema.

Soon, many mothers from the city wanted to go back home. Even the danger of bombs did not stop them going back.

▲ People cleaning up their home in the city after it was bombed.

Making friends

Some mothers made friends with their foster families. One woman said: 'We got on beautifully with our hosts, sharing a kitchen and all that and we're still in touch now, all these years later.'

Going Abroad

At the start of the war, some parents thought that nowhere in Britain was safe. So they sent their children abroad, to places far away from Britain. Many children went to Canada, Australia, South Africa and the USA.

One evacuee wrote of her stay in the USA: 'I had a jolly good six years. I found myself miles ahead of the American schoolchildren, so life was easy.'

▼ British evacuees starting their long voyage abroad.

The journey

Evacuees made long and dangerous voyages on ocean liners. One child wrote about a voyage to Australia which lasted eleven weeks: 'We were chased by submarines ... there was great homesickness and much seasickness, lifeboat drill and lots of singing.'

In 1940, the Germans sank a ship full of evacuees going to Canada. After that, most parents kept their children in Britain.

LEAVE THIS TO US SONNY — <u>YOU</u> OUGHT TO BE OUT OF LONDON

MINISTRY OF HEALTH EVACUATION SCHEME

▲ A British poster from 1942.

◄ Doctors examining children before they travel abroad.

Evacuated Again

▼ Houses damaged by German bombs.

In the first months of the war there was no bombing. Many evacuees went back to their homes. But in the summer of 1940, the Germans invaded France. Now they were very near to Britain. People started to evacuate their children again.

Barbed wire was put up along the south coast to stop German invaders.

People were afraid the Germans would cross the sea from France. Children were sent away from the south coast of England. Some children had already been evacuated to the south coast from London. Now they were moved again.

Bombs and rockets

German planes bombed Britain. During the Blitz, London was bombed night after night. Many people were killed. More children were evacuated to safety.

In 1944 and 1945 Germany used flying bombs and rockets to attack Britain. They did a lot of damage. More children had to be evacuated.

▲ The Germans fired rockets like this at Britain.

German Evacuees

Near the end of the war, the Russians got ready to invade Germany. The Germans decided to evacuate people from along the border with Russia.

Millions of German evacuees and injured soldiers travelled to ports in the north of Germany.

▼ German evacuees at the end of the war.

◄ German ships carrying evacuees.

The land was covered with deep snow. One German evacuee wrote: 'There were children who pulled their sick mothers along on sleighs or boards, searching for a doctor, a bed or just a warm corner.'

The end of the war

At the start of 1945 there was a terrible disaster. A Russian submarine sank a German ship carrying 8,000 German evacuees. Five times more people were killed than on the *Titanic*.

Ships evacuated over two million German people to other countries. In May 1945, the war in Europe ended.

▼ A painting of German evacuees leaving Berlin.

Glossary

Blitz The German bombing of London which began in 1940.

border The line between two countries.

cattle auction A sale, where cows are sold to the person offering the most money.

dripping Melted fat.

evacuate Move people away from danger to a safe place.

evacuee A person moved away from a dangerous place.

foster parents People who act as parents to children who are not their own.

invade Send an army into a foreign country.

Jewish Believing in a religion called Judaism.

lice Blood-sucking insects which live in people's hair and on people's skin.

lifeboat drill Practice in launching lifeboats.

ocean liners Large ships which carry passengers across oceans.

sensation A feeling.

sleighs Sledges for people to ride on through snow.

submarine A warship which can travel under water.

voyage A long journey by water or by air.

Projects

1 Talk to relatives and friends who were evacuated in 1939. These are some questions you can ask them:

- Did you go with your school?
- Where were you evacuated to?
- Who did you stay with?

2 Imagine that you have an evacuee staying in your home. Write about how you feel. Then write about how you think the evacuee feels.

Books to Read

Children of the Blitz by Robert Westall (Piccolo, 1995)

The Sandbag Secret – A Tale about the Blitz by Jon Blake (Franklin Watts, 1998)

Scotland in World War II by Richard Dargie (Wayland, 1997)

Places to Visit

Britain at War Experience, 64 Tooley Street, London. Tel: 0171 378 1147
Here, you can try on tin helmets, gas masks and uniforms.

Eden Camp, Malton, North Yorkshire. Tel: 01653 697777
This museum tells you about everyday life during World War II.

The Imperial War Museum, London. Tel: 0171 416 5313
This museum has displays all about World War II.

Use this book for teaching literacy

This book can help you in the literacy hour in the following ways:

✓ Children can use the contents page, page numbers, headings, captions and index to locate a particular piece of information.

✓ Posters, advertisements and newspaper headlines are good examples of the different styles of writing needed for Year 4 literacy teaching.

✓ Children can use the glossary to reinforce their alphabetic knowledge and extend their vocabulary.

✓ They can compare this book with fictional stories about evacuation to show how similar information can be presented in different ways.

Index

Numbers in **bold** refer to pictures and captions.